Contents

Introduction

The prevalence of chronic kidney disease (CKD) is high and it is gradually increasing. Individuals with CKD should introduce appropriate measures to hamper the progression of kidney function deterioration as well as prevent the development or progression of CKD-related diseases. A kidney-friendly diet may help to protect kidneys from further damage. Patients with kidney damage should limit the intake of certain foods to reduce the accumulation of unexcreted metabolic products and also to protect against hypertension, proteinuria and other heart and bone health problems. Despite the fact that the influence of certain types of nutrients has been widely studied in relation to kidney function and overall health in CKD patients, there are few studies on the impact of a specific diet on their survival. Animal studies demonstrated prolonged survival of rats with CKD fed with protein-restricted diets. In humans, the results of studies are conflicting. Some of them indicate slowing down of the progression of kidney disease and reduction in proteinuria, but other underline significant worsening of patients' nutritional state, which can be dangerous. A recent systemic study revealed that a healthy diet comprising many fruits and vegetables, fish, legumes, whole grains, and fibers and also the cutting down on red meat, sodium, and refined sugar intake was associated with lower mortality in people with kidney disease. The aim of this paper is to review the results of studies concerning the impact of diet on the survival of CKD patients.

The prevalence of chronic kidney disease (CKD) is high and it is gradually increasing. Persons with CKD should introduce appropriate measures to hamper the progression of kidney function deterioration as well as to prevent the development or progression of CKD-related diseases. Current guidelines for CKD management recommend dietary and lifestyle modifications, however, they have largely been based on general population studies. A kidney-friendly diet may help to protect kidneys from further damage. In early CKD stages the adoption of healthy diet might slow glomerular filtration rate (GFR) decline and decrease the prevalence of complete kidney failure. Patients with kidney damage should limit the intake of certain foods to reduce the accumulation of unexcreted metabolic products but also to protect against hypertension, proteinuria and other heart and bone health problems. Despite the fact that the influence of certain types of nutrients has been widely studied in relation to kidney function and overall health condition of CKD patients, there are few studies on the impact of specific diet on their survival.

The significance of proper diet in CKD is confirmed in a large retrospective cohort study of Slininetal. which demonstrated that the mortality rate of predialysis adult patients cared for by a dietitian was 19% lower in comparison to those who did not receive this care. It seems that nutritional treatment in early stages of CKD may prolong life; however, this hypothesis has not been assessed in a prospective randomized clinical trial. The

Third National Health and Nutrition Examination Survey (NHANES III) Linked Mortality File assessed the association between four lifestyle factors (diet, physical activity, body mass index—BMI, and smoking) with all-cause mortality among CKD participants. It demonstrated that individuals in the highest □uartile of the weighted healthy lifestyle score had a 53% lower risk of death compared with those in the lowest □uartile. Abstinence from smoking and regular versus no physical activity were associated with the highest reduction in mortality (46% and 20%, respectively), whereas a BMI of 18.5 to 22 kg/m2 was associated with a 30% increased mortality. Healthy diet, including high

intake of vegetables, fruits, nuts, whole grains, legumes, and fish and low in saturated fat and sodium was associated with lower rates of age-adjusted all-cause mortality in individuals with CKD. Beneficial effects of diet may be mediated by favorable effects on blood pressure (BP), glucose, and lipids. However, this relationship disappeared after adjustment for demographic factors. A plant-based diet was shown to influence survival through its impact on metabolic acidosis and blood pressure. Moreover, such a diet reduced urine parameters of kidney injury, decreased the production of potential uremic toxins through the alteration of gut flora, diminished body weight, and improved cardiovascular outcomes. On the other hand, high consumption of sugary drinks/sodas has been demonstrated to be associated with the incidence of albuminuria, CKD and faster GFR decline in the community. Moreover, a low-fructose diet was found in a randomized clinical trial to considerably reduce inflammatory biomarkers levels and blood pressure in comparison to a control group consuming a standard amount of fructose. revealed that adherence to a healthy lifestyle (including no smoking habits, low BMI, high physical activity and dietary quality) was associated with lower risk of all-cause mortality in people with stage 3 or more advanced CKD.

Kidney Disease

The kidneys are a pair of fist-sized organs located at the bottom of the rib cage. There is one kidney on each side of the spine. Kidneys are essential to having a healthy body. They are mainly responsible for filtering waste products, excess water, and other impurities out of the blood. These toxins are stored in the bladder and then removed during urination. The kidneys also regulate pH, salt, and potassium levels in the body. They produce hormones that regulate blood pressure and control the production of red blood cells. The kidneys even activate a form of vitamin D that helps the body absorb calcium. Kidney disease affects approximately 26 million American adults. It occurs when your kidneys become damaged and can't perform their function. Damage may be caused by diabetes, high blood pressure, and various other chronic (long-term) conditions. Kidney disease can lead to other health problems, including weak bones, nerve damage, and malnutrition. If the disease gets worse over time, your kidneys may stop working completely. This means that dialysis will be required to perform the function of the kidneys. Dialysis is a treatment that filters and purifies the blood using a machine. It can't cure kidney disease, but it can prolong your life.

Types and Causes of Kidney Disease

Chronic kidney disease

The most common form of kidney disease is chronic kidney disease. Chronic kidney disease is a long-term condition that doesn't improve over time. It's commonly caused by high blood pressure. High blood pressure is dangerous for the kidneys because it can increase the pressure on the glomeruli. Glomeruli are the tiny blood vessels in the kidneys where blood is cleaned. Over time, the increased pressure damages these vessels and kidney function begins to decline. Kidney function will eventually deteriorate to the point where the kidneys can no longer perform their job properly. In this case, a person would need to go on dialysis. Dialysis filters extra fluid and waste out of the blood. Dialysis can help treat kidney disease but it can't cure it. A kidney transplant may be another treatment option depending on your circumstances. Diabetes is also a major cause of chronic kidney disease. Diabetes is a group of diseases that causes high blood sugar. The increased level of sugar in the blood damages the blood vessels in the kidneys over time. This means the kidneys can't clean the blood properly. Kidney failure can occur when your body becomes overloaded with toxins.

Kidney stones

Kidney stones are another common kidney problem. They occur when minerals and other substances in the blood crystallize in the kidneys, forming solid masses (stones). Kidney stones usually come out of the body during urination. Passing kidney stones can be extremely painful, but they rarely cause significant problems.

Glomerulonephritis is an inflammation of the glomeruli. Glomeruli are extremely small structures inside the kidneys that filter the blood. Glomerulonephritis can be caused by infections, drugs, or congenital abnormalities (disorders that occur during or shortly after birth). It often gets better on its own.

Polycystic kidney disease is a genetic disorder that causes numerous cysts (small sacs of fluid) to grow in the kidneys. These cysts can interfere with kidney function and cause kidney failure. It's important to note that individual kidney cysts are fairly common and almost always harmless. Polycystic kidney disease is a separate, more serious condition.

Urinary tract infections (UTIs) are bacterial infections of any part of the urinary system. Infections in the bladder and urethra are the most common. They are easily treatable and rarely lead to more health problems. However, if left untreated, these infections can spread to the kidneys and cause kidney failure.

Symptoms of kidney disease

Kidney disease is a condition that can easily go unnoticed until the symptoms become severe. The following symptoms are early warning signs that you might be developing kidney disease:

• fatigue

• difficulty concentrating

• trouble sleeping

• poor appetite

• muscle cramping

• swollen feet/ankles

• puffiness around the eyes in the morning

• dry, scaly skin

• frequent urination, especially late at night

Severe symptoms that could mean your kidney disease is progressing into kidney failure include:

• nausea

• vomiting

• loss of appetite

• changes in urine output

• fluid retention

• anemia (a decrease in red blood cells)

• decreased sex drive

• sudden rise in potassium levels (hyperkalemia)

• inflammation of the pericardium (fluid-filled sac that covers the heart)

The risk factors for developing kidney disease

People with diabetes have a higher risk of developing kidney disease. Diabetes is the leading cause of kidney disease, accounting for about 44 percent of new cases. You may also be more likely to get kidney disease if you:

• Have high blood pressure

• Have other family members with chronic kidney disease

• Are elderly

• Are of African, Hispanic, Asian, or American Indian descent

How is kidney disease diagnosed

Your doctor will first determine whether you belong in any of the high-risk groups. They will then run some tests to see if your kidneys are functioning properly.

Glomerular filtration rate (GFR)

This test will measure how well your kidneys are working and determine the stage of kidney disease.

Ultrasound or computed tomography (CT) Scan

Ultrasounds and CT scans produce clear images of your kidneys and urinary tract. The pictures allow your doctor to see if your kidneys are too small or large. They can also show any tumors or structural problems that may be present.

Kidney biopsy

During a kidney biopsy, your doctor will remove a small piece of tissue from your kidney while you're sedated. The tissue sample can help your doctor determine the type of kidney disease you have and how much damage has occurred.

Urine test

Your doctor may re⬚uest a urine sample to test for albumin. Albumin is a protein that can be passed into your urine when your kidneys are damaged.

Blood creatinine test

Creatinine is a waste product. It's released into the blood when creatine (a molecule stored in muscle) is broken down. The levels of creatinine in your blood will increase if your kidneys aren't working properly.

How is kidney disease treated

Treatment for kidney disease usually focuses on controlling the underlying cause of the disease. This means your doctor will help you better manage your blood pressure, blood sugar, and cholesterol levels. They may use one or more of the following methods to treat kidney disease.

Drugs and medication

Your doctor will either prescribe angiotensin-converting enzyme (ACE) inhibitors, such as lisinopril and ramipril, or angiotensin receptor blockers (ARBs), such as irbesartan and olmesartan. These are blood pressure medications that can slow the progression of kidney disease. Your doctor may prescribe these medications to preserve kidney function, even if you don't have high blood pressure.

Dietary and lifestyle changes

Making changes to your diet is just as important as taking medication. Adopting a healthy lifestyle can help prevent many of the underlying causes of kidney disease. Your doctor may recommend that you:

• control diabetes through insulin injections

• cut back on foods high in cholesterol

• cut back on salt

- start a heart-healthy diet that includes fresh fruits, veggies, whole grains, and low-fat dairy products

- limit alcohol consumption

- quit smoking

- increase physical activity

- lose weight

Dialysis and kidney disease

Dialysis is an artificial method of filtering the blood. It's used when someone's kidneys have failed or are close to failing. Many people with late-stage kidney disease must go on dialysis permanently or until a donor kidney is found. There are two types of dialysis: hemodialysis and peritoneal dialysis.

Hemodialysis

In hemodialysis, the blood is pumped through a special machine that filters out waste products and fluid.

Hemodialysis is done at your home or in a hospital or dialysis center. Most people have three sessions per week, with each session lasting three to five hours. However, hemodialysis can also be done in shorter, more frequent sessions. Several weeks before starting hemodialysis, most people will have surgery to create an arteriovenous (AV) fistula. An AV fistula is created by connecting an artery and a vein just below the skin, typically in the forearm. The larger blood vessel allows an increased amount of blood to flow continuously through the body during hemodialysis treatment. This means more blood can be filtered and purified. An arteriovenous graft (a looped, plastic tube) may be implanted and used for the same purpose if an artery and vein can't be joined together. The most common side effects of hemodialysis are low blood pressure, muscle cramping, and itching.

In peritoneal dialysis, the peritoneum (membrane that lines the abdominal wall) stands in for the kidneys. A tube is implanted and used to fill the abdomen with a fluid called dialysate. Waste products in the blood flow from the peritoneum into the dialysate. The dialysate is then drained from the abdomen. There are two forms of peritoneal dialysis: continuous ambulatory peritonealdialysis, where the abdomen is filled and drained several times during the day, and continuous cycler-assisted peritoneal dialysis, which uses a machine to cycle the fluid in and out of the abdomen at night while the person sleeps. The most common side effects of peritoneal dialysis are infections in the abdominal cavity or in the area where the tube was implanted. Other side effects may include weight gain and hernias. A hernia is when the intestine pushes through a weak spot or tear in the lower abdominal wall.

The long-term outlook for someone with kidney disease

Kidney disease normally does not go away once it's diagnosed. The best way to maintain kidney health is to adopt a healthy lifestyle and follow your doctor's advice. Kidney disease can get worse over time. It may even lead to kidney failure. Kidney failure can be life-threatening if left untreated. Kidney failure occurs when your kidneys are barely working or not working at all. This is managed by dialysis. Dialysis involves the use of a machine to filter waste from your blood. In some cases, your doctor may recommend a kidney transplant.

How can kidney disease be prevented

Some risk factors for kidney disease such as age, race, or family history are impossible to control. However, there are measures you can take to help prevent kidney disease:

• drink plenty of water

• control blood sugar if you have diabetes

• control blood pressure

• reduce salt intake

• ⬚uit smoking

Be careful with over-the-counter drugs

You should always follow the dosage instructions for over-the-counter medications. Taking too much aspirin (Bayer) or ibuprofen (Advil, Motrin) can cause kidney damage.

Get tested

Kidney problems generally don't cause symptoms until they're more advanced. A basic metabolic panel (BMP) is a standard blood test that can be done as part of a routine medical exam. It checks your blood for creatinine or urea. These are chemicals that leak into the blood when the kidneys aren't working properly. A BMP can detect kidney problems early, when they're easier to treat. You should be tested annually if you have diabetes, heart disease, or high blood pressure.

Limit certain foods

Different chemicals in your food can contribute to certain types of kidney stones. These include:

- excessive sodium

- animal protein, such as beef and chicken

- citric acid, found in citrus fruits such as oranges, lemons, and grapefruits

- oxalate, a chemical found in beets, spinach, sweet potatoes, and chocolate

Kidney disease diet

Why is an eating plan important

What you eat and drink affects your health. Staying at a healthy weight and eating a balanced diet that is low in salt and fat can help you control your blood pressure. If you have diabetes, you can help control your blood sugar by carefully choosing what you eat and drink. Controlling high blood pressure and diabetes may help prevent kidney disease from getting worse. A kidney friendly diet may also help protect your kidneys from further damage. A kidney friendly diet limits certain foods to prevent the minerals in those foods from building up in your body.

Healthy diet basics

With all meal plans, including the kidney-friendly diet, you need to track how much of certain nutrients you take in, such as:

• Calories

• Protein

• Fat

• Carbohydrates

To make sure you are getting the right amounts of these nutrients, you need to eat and drink the right portion sizes. All of the information you need to keep track of your intake is on the "Nutrition Facts" label.

Use the nutrition facts section on food labels to learn more about what is in the foods you eat. The nutrition facts will tell you how much protein, carbohydrates, fat and sodium are in each serving of a food. This can help you pick foods that are high in the nutrients you need and low in the nutrients you should limit.

Calories

Your body gets energy from the calories you eat and drink. Calories come from the protein, carbohydrates and fat in your diet. How many calories you need depends on your age, gender, body size and activity level. You may also need to adjust how many calories you eat based on your weight goals. Some people will need to limit the calories they eat. Others may need to have more calories. Your doctor or dietitian can help you figure out how many calories you should have each day. Work with your dietitian to make a meal plan that helps you get the right amount of calories, and keep in touch for support.

Protein

Protein is one of the building blocks of your body. Your body needs protein to grow, heal and stay healthy. Having too little protein can cause your skin, hair and nails to be weak. But having too much protein can also be a problem. To stay healthy and help you feel your best, you may need to adjust how much protein you eat. The amount of protein you should have depends on your body size, activity level and health concerns. Some doctors recommend that people with kidney disease limit protein or change their source of protein. This is because a diet very high in protein can make the kidneys work harder and may cause more damage. Ask your doctor or dietitian how much protein you should have and what the best sources of protein are for you. Use the table below to learn which foods are low or high in protein. Keep in mind that just because a food is low in protein, it is not healthy to eat unlimited amounts.

Lower-protein foods:

• Bread

• Fruits

• Vegetables

• Pasta and rice

• Higher-protein foods:

• Red meat

• Poultry

• Fish

- Eggs

Carbohydrates

Carbohydrates ("carbs") are the easiest kind of energy for your body to use. Healthy sources of carbohydrates include fruits and vegetables. Unhealthy sources of carbohydrates include sugar, honey, hard candies, soft drinks and other sugary drinks. Some carbohydrates are high in potassium and phosphorus, which you may need to limit depending on your stage of kidney disease. We'll talk about this in more detail a little later. You may also need to watch your carbohydrates carefully if you have diabetes. Your dietitian can help you learn more about the carbohydrates in your meal plan and how they affect your blood sugar.

Fat

You need some fat in your meal plan to stay healthy. Fat gives you energy and helps you use some of the vitamins in your food. But too much fat can lead to weight gain and heart disease. Try to limit fat in your meal plan, and choose healthier fats when you can. Healthier fat or "good" fat is called unsaturated fat. Examples of unsaturated fat include:

• Olive oil

• Peanut oil

• Corn oil

Unsaturated fat can help reduce cholesterol. If you need to gain weight, try to eat more unsaturated fat. If you need to lose weight, limit the unsaturated fat in your meal plan. As always, moderation is the key. Too much "good" fat can also cause problems.

Saturated fat, also known as "bad" fat, can raise your cholesterol level and raise your risk for heart disease. Examples of saturated fats include:

• Butter

• Lard

• Shortening

Limit these in your meal plan. Choose healthier, unsaturated fat instead. Trimming the fat from meat and removing the skin from chicken or turkey can also help limit saturated fat. You should also avoid trans fat. This kind of fat makes your "bad" (LDL) cholesterol higher and your "good" (HDL) cholesterol lower. When this happens, you are more likely to get heart disease, which can cause kidney damage.

Sodium

Sodium (salt) is a mineral found in almost all foods. Too much sodium can make you thirsty, which can lead to swelling and raise your blood pressure. This can damage your kidneys more and make your heart work harder.

One of the best things that you can do to stay healthy is to limit how much sodium you eat. To limit sodium in your meal plan:

• Do not add salt to your food when cooking or eating. Try cooking with fresh herbs, lemon juice or other salt-free spices.

• Choose fresh or frozen vegetables instead of canned vegetables. If you do use canned vegetables, drain and rinse them to remove extra salt before cooking or eating them.

• Avoid processed meats like ham, bacon, sausage and lunch meats.

• Munch on fresh fruits and vegetables rather than crackers or other salty snacks.

• Avoid canned soups and frozen dinners that are high in sodium.

• Avoid pickled foods, like olives and pickles.

• Limit high-sodium condiments like soy sauce, BBQ sauce and ketchup.

Portions.

Choosing healthy foods is a great start, but eating too much of anything, even healthy foods, can be a problem. The other part of a healthy diet is portion control, or watching how much you eat.

To help control your portions:

• Check the nutrition facts label on a food to learn the serving size and how much of each nutrient is in one serving. Many packages have more than one serving. For example, a 20-ounce bottle of soda is really two-and-a-half servings. Many fresh foods, such as fruits and vegetables, do not come with nutrition facts labels. Ask your dietitian for a list of nutrition facts for fresh foods and tips for how to measure the right portions.

• Eat slowly, and stop eating when you are not hungry any more. It takes about 20 minutes for your stomach to tell your brain that you are full. If you eat too quickly, you may eat more than you need.

• Avoid eating while doing something else, such as watching TV or driving. When you are distracted you may not realize how much you have eaten.

• Do not eat directly from the package the food came in. Instead, take out one serving of food and put the bag or box away.

• Good portion control is an important part of any meal plan. It is even more important in a kidney-friendly meal plan, because you may need to limit how much of certain things you eat and drink.

How is a kidney friendly diet different

When your kidneys are not working as well as they should, waste and fluid build up in your body. Over time, the waste and extra fluid can cause heart, bone and other health problems. A kidney friendly meal plan limits how much of certain minerals and fluid you eat and drink. This can help keep the waste and fluid from building up and causing problems.

How strict your meal plan should be depends on your stage of kidney disease. In the early stages of kidney disease, you may have little or no limits on what you eat and drink. As your kidney disease gets worse, your doctor may recommend that you limit:

• Potassium

• Phosphorus

• Fluids

Potassium

Potassium is a mineral found in almost all foods. Your body needs some potassium to make your muscles work, but too much potassium can be dangerous. When your kidneys are not working well, your potassium level may be too high or too low. Having too much or too little potassium can cause muscle cramps, problems with the way your heart beats and muscle weakness. If you have kidney disease, you may need to limit how much potassium you take in. Use the list below to learn which foods are low or high in potassium:

• Apples, cranberries, grapes, pineapples and strawberries

• Cauliflower, onions, peppers, radishes, summer s🞎uash, lettuce

• Pita, tortillas and white breads

• Beef and chicken, white rice

• Higher potassium foods

• Avocados, bananas, melons, oranges, prunes and raisins

• Artichokes, winter squash, plantains, spinach, potatoes and tomatoes

• Bran products and granola

• Beans (baked, black, pinto, etc.), brown or wild rice

Phosphorus

Phosphorus is a mineral found in almost all foods. It works with calcium and vitamin D to keep your bones healthy. Healthy kidneys keep the right amount of phosphorus in your body. When your kidneys are not working well, phosphorus can build up in your blood. Too much phosphorus in your blood can lead to weak bones that break easily. Many people with kidney disease need to limit phosphorus.

Depending on your stage of kidney disease, your doctor may also prescribe a medicine called a phosphate binder. This helps to keep phosphorus from building up in your blood. A phosphate binder can be helpful, but you will still need to watch how much phosphorus you eat.

Use the list below to get some ideas about how to make healthy choices if you need to limit phosphorus:

• Italian, French or sourdough bread

• Corn or rice cereals and cream of wheat

- Unsalted popcorn

- Some light-colored sodas and lemonade

- Higher phosphorous foods

- Whole-grain bread

- Bran cereals and oatmeal

- Nuts and sunflower seeds

- Dark-colored colas

- Fluids

You need water to live, but when you have kidney disease, you may not need as much. This is because damaged kidneys do not get rid of extra fluid as well as they should. Too much fluid in your body can be dangerous. It can cause high blood pressure, swelling and heart failure. Extra fluid can also build up around your lungs and make it hard to breathe. Depending on your stage of kidney disease and your treatment, your doctor may tell you to limit fluid. Many fruits and vegetables are high in water, too.

If you do need to limit fluids, measure your fluids and drink from small cups to help you keep track of how much you've had to drink. Limit sodium to help cut down on thirst. At times, you may still feel thirsty. To help quench your thirst, you might try to:

• Chew gum

• Rinse your mouth

• Suck on a piece of ice, mints or hard candy (Remember to choose sugar-free candy if you have diabetes.

Special diet concerns

Vitamins

Following a kidney-friendly meal plan may make it hard for you to get all of the vitamins and minerals you need. To help you get the right amounts of vitamins and minerals. Regular multi-vitamins may not be healthy for you if you have kidney disease. They may have too much of some vitamins and not enough of others.

Food to eat for kidney disease patient

Kidney disease is a common problem affecting about 10% of the world's population. The kidneys are small but powerful bean-shaped organs that perform many important functions. They are responsible for filtering waste products, releasing hormones that regulate blood pressure, balancing fluids in the body, producing urine, and many other essential task. There are various ways in which these vital organs can become damaged.

Diabetes and high blood pressure are the most common risk factors for kidney disease. However, obesity, smoking, genetics, gender, and age can also increase the risk. Uncontrolled blood sugar and high blood pressure cause damage to blood vessels in the kidneys, reducing their ability to function optimally. When the kidneys aren't working properly, waste builds up in the blood, including waste products from food. Therefore, it's necessary for people with kidney disease to follow a special diet.

Diet and kidney disease

Dietary restrictions vary depending on the level of kidney damage. For example, people in the early stages of kidney disease have different restrictions than those with kidney failure, also known as end-stage renal disease (ESRD). For most people with advanced kidney disease, it's important to follow a kidney-friendly diet that helps decrease the amount of waste in the blood. This diet is often referred to as a renal diet, It helps boost kidney function while preventing further damage.

While dietary restrictions vary, it's commonly recommended that all people with kidney disease restrict the following nutrients:

• Sodium. Sodium is found in many foods and a major component of table salt. Damaged kidneys can't filter out excess sodium, causing its blood levels to rise. It's often recommended to limit sodium to less than 2,000 mg per day.

• Potassium. Potassium plays many critical roles in the body, but those with kidney disease need to limit potassium to avoid dangerously high blood levels. It's usually recommended to limit potassium to less than 2,000 mg per day.

• Phosphorus. Damaged kidneys can't remove excess phosphorus, a mineral in many foods. High levels can cause damage to the body, so dietary phosphorus is restricted to less than 800–1,000 mg per day in most patients.

• Protein is another nutrient that people with kidney disease may need to limit, as damaged kidneys can't clear out waste products from protein metabolism.

However, those with end-stage renal disease undergoing dialysis, a treatment that filters and cleans the blood, have greater protein needs. Each person with kidney disease is different, which is why it's important to talk to your healthcare provider about your individual dietary needs. Luckily, many delicious and healthy options are low in phosphorus, potassium, and sodium.

Best foods for people with kidney disease.
1.Cauliflower

Cauliflower is a nutritious vegetable that's a good source of many nutrients, including vitamin C, vitamin K, and the B vitamin folate, It's also full of anti-inflammatory compounds like indoles and is an excellent source of fiber. Plus, mashed cauliflower can be used in place of potatoes for a low potassium side dish.

One cup (124 grams) of cooked cauliflower contains:

• sodium: 19 mg

• potassium: 176 mg

• phosphorus: 40 mg

2. Blueberries

Blueberries are packed with nutrients and one of the best sources of antioxidants you can eat. In particular, these sweet berries contain antioxidants called anthocyanins, which may protect against heart disease, certain cancers, cognitive decline, and diabetes. They also make a fantastic addition to a kidney-friendly diet, as they are low in sodium, phosphorus, and potassium.

One cup (148 grams) of fresh blueberries contains:

- sodium: 1.5 mg

- potassium: 114 mg

- phosphorus: 18 mg

3. Sea bass

Sea bass is a high quality protein that contains incredibly healthy fats called omega-3s. Omega-3s help reduce inflammation and may help decrease the risk of cognitive decline, depression, and anxiety. While all fish are high in phosphorus, sea bass contains lower amounts than other seafood. However, it's important to consume small portions to keep your phosphorus levels in check.

Three ounces (85 grams) of cooked sea bass contain:

• sodium: 74 mg

• potassium: 279 mg

• phosphorus: 211 mg

4. Red grapes

Red grapes are not only delicious but also deliver a ton of nutrition in a small package. They're high in vitamin C and contain antioxidants called flavonoids, which have been shown to reduce inflammation.

Additionally, red grapes are high in resveratrol, a type of flavonoid that has been shown to benefit heart health and protect against diabetes and cognitive decline.

These sweet fruits are kidney-friendly, with a half cup (75 grams) containing:

• sodium: 1.5 mg

• potassium: 144 mg

• phosphorus: 15 mg

5. Egg whites

Although egg yolks are very nutritious, they contain high amounts of phosphorus, making egg whites a better choice for people following a renal diet. Egg whites provide a high quality, kidney-friendly source of protein. Plus, they're an excellent choice for people undergoing dialysis treatment, who have higher protein needs but need to limit phosphorus.

Two large egg whites (66 grams) contain:

• sodium: 110 mg

• potassium: 108 mg

• phosphorus: 10 mg

6. Garlic

People with kidney problems are advised to limit the amount of sodium in their diet, including added salt. Garlic provides a delicious alternative to salt, adding flavor to dishes while providing nutritional benefits, It's a good source of manganese, vitamin C, and vitamin B6 and contains sulfur compounds that have anti-inflammatory properties.

Three cloves (9 grams) of garlic contain:

• sodium: 1.5 mg

• potassium: 36 mg

• phosphorus: 14 mg

7. Buckwheat

Many whole grains tend to be high in phosphorus, but buckwheat is a healthy exception. Buckwheat is highly nutritious, providing a good amount of B vitamins, magnesium, iron, and fiber, It's also a gluten-free grain, making buckwheat a good choice for people with celiac disease or gluten intolerance.

A half cup (84 grams) of cooked buckwheat contains:

• sodium: 3.5 mg

• potassium: 74 mg

• phosphorus: 59 mg

8. Olive oil

Olive oil is a healthy source of fat and phosphorus-free, making it a great option for people with kidney disease. Frequently, people with advanced kidney disease have trouble keeping weight on, making healthy, high calorie foods like olive oil important. The majority of fat in olive oil is a monounsaturated fat called oleic acid, which has anti-inflammatory properties. Monounsaturated fats are stable at high temperatures, making olive oil a healthy choice for cooking.

One tablespoon (13.5 grams) of olive oil contains:

• sodium: 0.3 mg

• potassium: 0.1 mg

• phosphorus: 0 mg

9. Bulgur

Bulgur is a whole grain wheat product that makes a terrific, kidney-friendly alternative to other whole grains that are high in phosphorus and potassium. This nutritious grain is a good source of B vitamins, magnesium, iron, and manganese, It's also an excellent source of plant-based protein and full of dietary fiber, which is important for digestive health.

A half-cup (91-gram) serving of bulgur contains:

• sodium: 4.5 mg

• potassium: 62 mg

• phosphorus: 36 mg

10. Cabbage

Cabbage belongs to the cruciferous vegetable family and is loaded with vitamins, minerals, and powerful plant compounds, It's a great source of vitamin K, vitamin C, and many B vitamins.

Furthermore, it provides insoluble fiber, a type of fiber that keeps your digestive system healthy by promoting regular bowel movements and adding bulk to stool.

Plus, it's low in potassium, phosphorus, and sodium, with one cup (70 grams) of shredded cabbage containing:

• sodium: 13 mg

- potassium: 119 mg

- phosphorus: 18 mg

11. Skinless chicken

Although a limited protein intake is necessary for some people with kidney issues, providing the body with an adequate amount of high quality protein is vital for health. Skinless chicken breast contains less phosphorus, potassium, and sodium than skin-on chicken. When shopping for chicken, choose fresh chicken and avoid pre-made roasted chicken, as it contains large amounts of sodium and phosphorus. Three ounces (84 grams) of skinless chicken breast contains:

- sodium: 63 mg

- potassium: 216 mg

- phosphorus: 192 mg

12. Bell peppers

Bell peppers contain an impressive amount of nutrients but are low in potassium, unlike many other vegetables. These brightly colored peppers are loaded with the powerful antioxidant vitamin C. In fact, one small red bell pepper (74 grams) contains 105% of the recommended intake of vitamin C. They are also loaded with vitamin A, an important nutrient for immune function, which is often compromised in people with kidney disease.

One small red pepper (74 grams) contains:

• sodium: 3 mg

• potassium: 156 mg

• phosphorus: 19 mg

13. Onions

Onions are excellent for providing sodium-free flavor to renal-diet dishes. Reducing salt intake can be challenging, making finding flavorful salt alternatives a must. Sautéing onions with garlic and olive oil adds flavor to dishes without compromising your kidney health. Onions are high in vitamin C, manganese, and B vitamins and contain prebiotic fibers that help keep your digestive system healthy by feeding beneficial gut bacteria.

One small onion (70 grams) contains:

• sodium: 3 mg

• potassium: 102 mg

• phosphorus: 20 mg

14. Arugula

Many healthy greens like spinach and kale are high in potassium and difficult to fit into a renal diet. However, arugula is a nutrient-dense green that is low in potassium, making it a good choice for kidney friendly salads and side dishes. Arugula is a good source of vitamin K and the minerals manganese and calcium, all of which are important for bone health. This nutritious green also contains nitrates, which have been shown to lower blood pressure, an important benefit for those with kidney disease.

One cup (20 grams) of raw arugula contains:

• sodium: 6 mg

• potassium: 74 mg

• phosphorus: 10 mg

15. Macadamia nuts

Most nuts are high in phosphorus and not recommended for those following a renal diet. However, macadamia nuts are a delicious option for people with kidney problems. They are much lower in phosphorus than popular nuts like peanuts and almonds. They are also packed with healthy fats, B vitamins, magnesium, copper, iron, and manganese.

One ounce (28 grams) of macadamia nuts contains:

• sodium: 1.4 mg

• potassium: 103 mg

• phosphorus: 53 mg

Foods to avoid

There are several foods that people should avoid if they want to improve their kidney health or prevent damage to these organs.

These include the following:

• Phosphorous-rich foods

• Too much phosphorus can put stress on the kidneys. Research has shown that there is a correlation between high phosphorous intake and an increased risk of long-term damage to the kidneys.

However, there is not enough evidence to prove that phosphorous causes this damage, so more research into this topic is necessary.

For people looking to reduce their phosphorous intake, foods high in phosphorous include:

• meat

• dairy products

• most grains

• legumes

• nuts

• fish

Red meat

Some types of protein may be harder for the kidneys, or the body in general, to process. These include red meat. Initial research has shown that people who eat a lot of red meat have a higher risk of end-stage kidney disease than those who eat less red meat. However, there is a need for more studies to investigate this risk.

Foods for people with CKD

Cabbage may be beneficial for people with CKD. While the above foods may support a healthy kidney in general, they are not usually the best choices for people with CKD. Doctors will put most people with CKD on a specific diet to avoid minerals that the kidneys process, such as sodium, potassium, and phosphorous. The National Institute of Diabetes and Digestive and Kidney Diseases recommend that people with CKD eat less than 2,300 milligrams of sodium each day.

As CKD progresses, people may also need to limit their phosphorous intake, as this mineral can build up in the blood of people with this disease. Choosing the right amount of potassium is also important for people with CKD, as problems may occur when potassium levels get too high or low. People with CKD should aim to eat healthful foods that are low in these minerals but still provide the body with other nutrients. It may also be important for people with CKD to reduce their protein intake and only include small amounts of protein in their meals. When the body uses protein, it turns into waste, which the kidneys must then filter out, eating a diet lower in protein may protect against complications of CKD, such as metabolic acidosis, which occurs as kidney function deteriorates. The researchers indicated that eating a diet rich in fruits and vegetables and low in protein might help reduce these risks. People with CKD can work directly with a dietitian to create a suitable diet plan that meets their needs.

Cabbage

Cabbage is a leafy vegetable that may be beneficial for people with CKD. It is relatively low in potassium and very low in sodium, yet it also contains many helpful compounds and vitamins.

Red bell peppers

In addition to being very low in minerals such as sodium and potassium, red bell peppers contain helpful antioxidant compounds, which may protect the cells from damage.

Garlic

Garlic is an excellent seasoning choice for people with CKD. It can give other foods a more satisfying, full flavor, which may reduce the need for extra salt. Garlic also offers a range of health benefits.

Cauliflower

Cauliflower is a versatile vegetable for people with CKD. With the right preparation, it makes a good replacement for foods such as rice, mashed potatoes, and even pizza crust. Cauliflower also contains a range of nutrients without providing too much sodium, potassium, or phosphorous.

Arugula

People with CKD may have to avoid many greens, but arugula can be a great replacement. Arugula is generally lower in potassium than other greens, but it still contains fiber and other beneficial nutrients.

Berries

Blueberries are a healthful snack for people with CKD. The fruits below can be a healthful sweet snack for people with CKD:

- cranberries

- strawberries

- blueberries

- raspberries

- red grapes

- cherries

Olive oil

Olive oil may be the best cooking oil because of the type of fat that it contains. Olive oil is high in oleic acid, which is a polyunsaturated fatty acid that may help reduce inflammation in the body.

Egg whites

Eggs are a simple protein, but the yolks are very high in phosphorous. People with CKD can make omelets or scrambled eggs using just the egg whites.

Foods for people with CKD to avoid

For people with CKD, some foods may be difficult for the body to process and might place more stress on the kidney. These include:

- white potatoes

- red meat

- dairy products

- sugary beverages

- avocado

- bananas

- canned foods

- pickled foods

• alcohol

• egg yolks

People looking to protect their kidneys from future damage may also want to consider eating these foods in moderation.

Kidney disease diet recipe

Kidney diet menu: Day 1

Breakfast

- Ziptop Omelet
- English muffin or toasted bread
- Jam or jelly, margarine or butter
- Fresh grapes
- Coffee or tea
- Sweetener or creamer

Lunch

- Blackened shrimp pineapple salad
- Low-sodium crackers or crisp bread
- Lemon cookies
- Lemon-lime soda

Dinner

- Stuffed green peppers

- Dinner rolls

- Margarine or butter

- Stuffed strawberries

- Sparkling water

Day 1 tips:

• Adjust Ziptop Omelet recipe for the number of omelets you plan to serve. You can make extra to refrigerate for an even Quicker breakfast the next day. Reheat in the microwave for 20 to 30 seconds.

• Increase shrimp in the salad if you are on a higher protein diet. Use leftover shrimp to make shrimp spread with crackers for a snack.

• Make lemon cookies and serve as dessert at lunch or for an in-between-meals snack.

• Buy grapes to serve at breakfast they can be used for the second day's salad and for the third day's dinner, dessert or snack.

• Use the extra pineapple as a snack or a dessert if you have leftovers once you make the blackened shrimp pineapple salad.

• Buy enough strawberries for the stuffed strawberries recipe, the second day's pancake recipe and snacks, if desired.

• Leftover stuffed peppers are easy to refrigerate or freeze for a quick lunch or dinner later in the week.

Breakfast

- Egg in a Hole
- Homemade Pan Sausage
- Toasted bread
- Jam or jelly, margarine or butter
- Pineapple juice

Lunch

- Tuna veggie salad
- Sliced bread or pita bread
- Lemon cookies
- Home-brewed iced tea with lemon and sweetener

Dinner

- Slow rotisserie-style chicken
- Red wine vinaigrette asparagus

- Pasta tossed in olive oil and garlic

- Chilled or frozen grapes

- Decaffeinated coffee or herb tea

Day 2 tips:

• Make a batch of Homemade Pan Sausage and freeze patties on waxed paper and place in a freezer bag. You can prepare individual servings Quickly throughout the week.

• Tuna veggie salad calls for steamed vegetables, but you can add uncooked veggies if desired.

• Home-brewed iced tea tastes fresh and is free of phosphate additives compared to some canned or bottled prepared teas.

• Use leftover chicken from dinner for third day's lunch salad.

Kidney diet menu: Day 3

Breakfast

- Cottage cheese pancakes with fresh strawberries
- Whipped topping or syrup
- Scrambled egg or egg whites
- Coffee or tea
- Sweetener or creamer

Lunch

- Lemon curry chicken salad
- Naan (Indian flatbread) or pita bread
- Cranberry juice

Dinner

- Cilantro-lime cod
- Lettuce, cucumber and carrot salad
- Basic salad dressing
- Steamed Rice

- Luscious Lime Dessert

- Lemon-lime soda

Day 3 tips:

• Include the eggs if you need a higher protein breakfast. Use low-cholesterol eggs or egg whites only if you are concerned about cholesterol. Egg whites are very low in phosphorus.

• If you have time, make the lemon curry chicken salad the evening before so flavors can blend together.

• Look for fresh cod or any comparable white fish on sale this week. You can also use frozen cod, sole or halibut.

• The basic salad dressing recipe has only one milligram of sodium for two tablespoons, compared to 250 to 400 mg for commercially prepared salad dressing. It will keep for several weeks in the refrigerator.

• To jazz up steamed rice, add your favorite low-sodium herb seasoning blend. Make extra rice for a kidney-friendly fried rice dish later in the week.

Conclusion

Chronic kidney disease-mineral and bone disorder (CKD-MBD) is a systemic dysfunction of mineral and bone metabolism in patients with CKD. It results from abnormalities in calcium, phosphorous, parathyroid hormone and/or vitamin D metabolism as well as abnormalities in bone turnover, mineralization, volume, linear growth or strength, in addition to vascular or other soft tissue calcification. Phosphate retention plays a crucial role in the development of CKD-MBD and it also increases the risk of cardiovascular events and mortality in patients with CKD. In the early stages of CKD serum phosphate levels are maintained in the normal range through phosphaturia induced by increase in parathyroid hormone actions and fibroblast growth factor-23 production. However, as kidney disease progresses the compensatory rise in FGF-23 levels fails to sustain phosphate clearance sufficiently and hyperphosphatemia ensues. Notably, increased FGF-23 levels by itself has been associated with increases in both cardiovascular events and mortality, suggesting that control of phosphate homeostasis early in CKD may help reducing the clinical consequences of mineral and bone disorders. Strategies to manage elevated serum phosphorus levels include reduction of dietary phosphate intake, as well as the use of phosphate binding agents. Clinical studies have assessed the effects of dietary phosphate and protein restriction in CKD patients. For example, patients with advanced CKD (stages 4 and 5) who had a reduction in dietary phosphates and protein intake also had improved short-term control of secondary hyperparathyroidism. In the long term, altering the diet allowed some patients to achieve a normal rate of bone formation. Recent evidence suggests that in addition to the absolute amount of phosphate in the diet, its source (i.e., plant versus animal food) should be considered. Indeed, dietary phosphates from plant-derived proteins are mostly in the form of phytates, which are less digestible in humans. We conclude that integrating dietary manipulations into a comprehensive strategy will help prevent or ameliorate complications of CKD including acidosis, hyperkalemia, hyperphosphatemia and uremic symptoms and possibly influence CKD progression. We believe particular attention should be paid. To correcting metabolic acidosis with either sodium bicarbonate supplements or more simply with diet instructions how to include supplements of fruits and vegetables and to lower the intake of sodium chloride as well as phosphates by choosing foods that provide low contents of these ions. Changing the diet by concentrating on these dietary constituents will allow us to maximize the renoprotective anti-proteinuric effect of renin angiotensin system blockers. These considerations on dietary approaches for CKD prevention and management are particularly valuable for low-resource setting worldwide where patients with CKD are beset with numerous challenges often traceable to poverty and a lack of access to life-saving dialysis and transplantation. The feasibility of these management approaches for CKD and its risk factors even in low-income countries is exemplified by the program set up in the communities of Eastern Nepal in collaboration with the International Society of Nephrology (ISN). Dietary recommendation of low-sodium intake and increase of fruits and vegetable together with low-cost anti-hypertensive, anti-diabetic or renoprotective drugs as deemed appropriate, have been able to control proteinuria and slow renal function decline in more than a third of 3,400 individuals on active monitoring.

Regarding the very low protein diet with essential keto acids and amino acids regimen, there is recent and reassuring evidence for its efficacy and nutritionally safety but efforts are needed to improve compliance with dietary regimens. Nutritional educational programs and dieticians could help to increase patient adherence to dietary recommendations. We also recommend that components of the diet and regular monitoring of nutritional status should be jointly assessed by physicians and dieticians, just as recommended for patients with inherited metabolic defects, cirrhosis and diabetes.